Homes

Elizabeth Nonweiler

raintree

yurt

teepee

rounded huts

Alcazar

Interesting facts about the pictures

page 2: A **yurt** has a frame of bent wood covered with felt made from sheep's wool. It is home for nomads (people who move with their animals) in Central Asia. They take it apart to move.

page 3: **Teepees** were the homes of some tribes of people in America. They were made of wooden poles and animal skins in the shape of a cone. They were warm, dry and easy to pack away.

page 4: These **rounded huts** are the homes of the El Molo tribe of Kenya in Africa. They are made from wood and palm tree leaves and built on the shores of a lake.

page 5: These **mud brick homes** are more than 1,000 years old. They belong to the Pueblo people of North America. They had no doors at first, only holes in the roof. The people got in and out by climbing ladders.

page 6: These **straw homes** are on an island on Lake Titicaca in South America. The island is made of soft floating reeds that grow in the lake and the houses are made of dry straw from the reeds.

page 7: This **home** has **stone** walls and a roof of **thatch** (dried plants like straw) to keep rain out. It is on a croft, a piece of land for growing vegetables. Now homes like this are often used for holidays.

page 8: This building used to be a **barn** for animals or for storing grain or hay, but now it is a home for people. It has been **converted** (changed) by adding windows, walls, a kitchen and so on.

page 9: A **mobile home** can be moved from one place to another, either towed or on a trailer. It may be used for holidays or by travelling people, or it may be a house taken to one place to stay there.

page 10: An **apartment block**, or block of flats, has lots of homes in one tall building. Sometimes the people share a laundry and a car park. In Finland they share a sauna, a very hot room to relax in.

page 11: **Sandstone tenements** have lots of homes in one building too. They were built in Victorian times and are common in cities in Scotland. Each entrance has stairs to several homes.

page 12: These **underground homes** are in Tunisia in Africa. First a big pit was dug out. Then homes were made by digging caves for rooms and passages to connect them.

page 13: **Alcazar** is built on a rocky hill in Spain. It was a home for kings, and also a fort to keep out enemies, a prison and a military school. Now it is a museum, with amazing rooms and paintings.

Letter-sound correspondences

Level 2 books cover the following letter-sound correspondences.
Letter-sound correspondences highlighted in **green** can be found in this book.

ant	**b**ig	**c**at	**d**og	**e**gg	**f**ish	**g**et	**h**ot	**i**t
jet	**k**ey	**l**et	**m**an	**n**ut	**o**ff	**p**an	**qu**een	**r**un
sun	**t**ap	**u**p	**v**an	**w**et	bo**x**	**y**es	**z**oo	
du**ck**	fi**sh**	**ch**ips	si**ng**	**th**in **th**is	k**ee**p	l**oo**k m**oo**n	**ar**t	c**or**n

s**ay**	b**oy**	r**ai**n	**oi**l	b**oa**t	**ea**t	p**ie**	h**igh**
m**a**k**e**	th**e**s**e**	l**i**k**e**	n**o**t**e**	fl**u**t**e** t**u**b**e**	**ou**t	s**aw**	**au**thor
h**er**	b**ir**d	t**ur**n	**air**port	fl**ew** st**ew**	bl**ue** c**ue**	**ph**one	**wh**en